Conquering has more to do with my tenacity than my abilities

© Copyright 2021 Stephanie M Captain

Chasing rumors is like

standing on quick sand

© Copyright 2021 Stephanie M Captain

Holding on to the past is giving

up your permission to the future

© Copyright 2021 Stephanie M Captain

In life, lessons are ongoing.

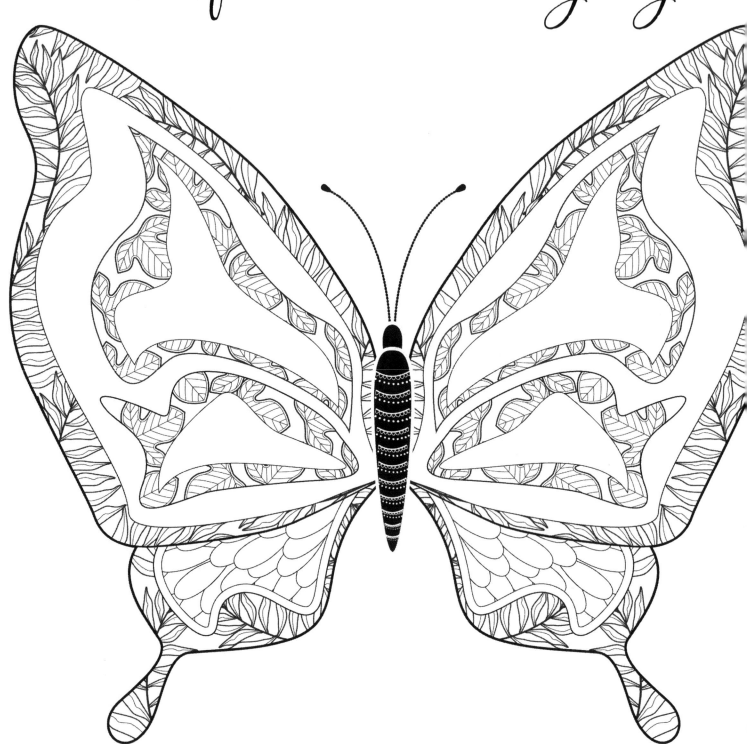

You must choose to be a student

© Copyright 2021 Stephanie M Captain

Some people bring shade, others bring heat

But you are the only one that controls the thermostat

© Copyright 2021 Stephanie M Captain

I must spend more time each day focusing on what is right in my life instead of what is wrong or who has wronged me

© Copyright 2021 Stephanie M Captain

I am my greatest influence

Some people judge you for who you are, others judge you for where you have been,

few can see where you are going

© Copyright 2021 Stephanie M Captain

love doesn't use a measuring stick

You can't catch the wind

but you can allow it to carry you

© Copyright 2021 Stephanie M Captain

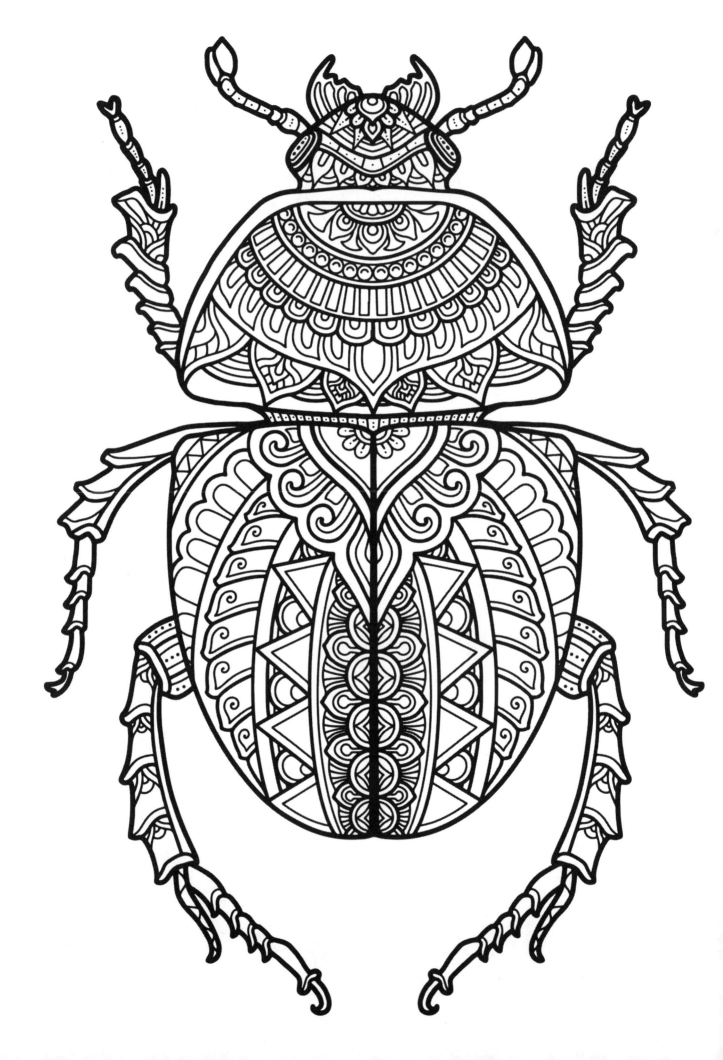

The best way to move on

is to move on

If you learn to choose your battles,

you won't always be winded

Don't apologize for being you

© Copyright 2021 Stephanie M Captain

Worry is an abuser and

fear is a thief

© Copyright 2021 Stephanie M Captain

All rights reserved. Copyright Stephanie M. Captain P.O. Box 7713; Augusta, Georgia 30905.

Made in the USA
Columbia, SC
11 February 2021